T0194807

Nuggets for the Soul

MARY MOORE JORDAN

WESTBOW
PRESS®
A DIVISION OF THOMAS NELSON
& ZONDERVAN

This book is a work of non-fiction. Unless otherwise noted, the author
and the publisher make no explicit guarantees as to the accuracy of
the information contained in this book and in some cases, names
of people and places have been altered to protect their privacy.

WestBow Press books may be ordered through booksellers or by contacting:

WestBow Press
A Division of Thomas Nelson & Zondervan
1663 Liberty Drive
Bloomington, IN 47403
www.westbowpress.com
844-714-3454

ISBN: 978-1-6642-5930-0 (sc)
ISBN: 978-1-6642-5929-4 (hc)
ISBN: 978-1-6642-5931-7 (e)

Library of Congress Control Number: 2022903986

Print information available on the last page.

WestBow Press rev. date: 03/24/2022

Clarence Larkin, Dispensational Truth (Glenside, PA: Rev. Clarence Larkin Publishers, 1918) 99. Used with permission of the Rev. Clarence Larkin Estate, PO Box 334, Glenside, PA 19038 (8/24/21), www.larkinestate.com.

Cover concept by Joan Jordan-Woolard

The whole book *Nuggets for the Soul* is filled with biblical nuggets that if every student knew them, we would have a better world. What compelling messengers you are—I love that this book will make an incredible mark on the reader. Follow the principles; they will take you from where you are to where you want to be.

Bishop James E. Jordan Jr., Pastor
Refreshing Spring Church of God in Christ
Riverdale, Maryland

The spiritual words of wisdom found in *Nuggets for the Soul* awaken the true meaning of life within us. We live in uncertain times and need the inspiration of the nuggets to find a spirit of peace, joy, love, and wisdom as we walk through each day. Let your emotions, mind, and will bless your soul as you read through the nuggets.
God bless you,

Kathy Moore
Freedom Fellowship
Virginia Beach, Virginia

In Memory of My Grandmother

"Nana," Dorothy L. Thompson, was the greatest evangelist missionary I have known. She loved her family and spent time teaching us how to search the scripture for daily application. She touched many lives, feeding hungry souls spiritually and naturally while ministering in churches, parks, streets, and shelters. I thank God for her love and influence in my life to remain steadfast and unmovable, always abounding in the work of the Lord.

Acknowledgments

Deacon Charles K. Jordan
Evangelist Sheila Outlaw
Jacqueline Jones
Ladonna Fennell
Clifford Moore
Mother Herldleen Russell
Mother Joan Jordan Woolard
Dr. Frederick Ware
Pastor, Mother Cloretta Grice
Mother Wilhelmenia Irene Jordan

Contents

Foreword

Christian spiritual formation is a process of becoming Christlike in character and conduct for the glory of God and the sake of other persons. The definition makes spiritual formation sound simple. In reality, the process is challenging. Believers do not know instinctively what to do. However, we are not without help. God is gracious and provides guidance.

Mary Moore Jordan's *Nuggets for the Soul* is one of God's gifts of grace to the believer. She calls the believer's attention to the soul—that precious part of the human person beyond the representation of ourselves and other persons as mere biological organisms. To be human is to be both body and soul. Human well-being, if it is to be achieved and maintained, requires that our physical needs be pursued in the light of wisdom for the nurture of mind, will, and emotion.

The expressions of wisdom that Mary Jordan calls "nuggets" are presented plainly but profoundly with vivid illustrations and practical applications. In this book, the reader will find thought-provoking ideas, principles of action, and exercises for the implementation of both in Christian living. In as much as other Christian authors have written on the topic of spiritual and moral formation, I find it refreshing to see a book like Mary Jordan's that reflects a Pentecostal-holiness perspective informed by years of life experience, exemplary ministerial service, and careful study.

Frederick L. Ware, PhD
Professor of Theology and Associate Dean for Academic Affairs
Howard University School of Divinity
Washington, DC

Introduction

There is a treasure to be desired and
oil in the dwelling of the wise.

Proverbs 21:20

What are "nuggets"? Nuggets are defined here as scriptural words of wisdom. In this handy book titled *Nuggets for the Soul,* you will find valuable treasures from the Bible that will explain, inform, and inspire believers in Christ Jesus on how to prosper and be in health spiritually and naturally on this journey called life. This book provides you with practical living strategies to help build up the soul during difficult times to overcome the challenges and disappointments that tend to arise in life.

I am an educator, minister, and certified lay healthcare chaplain. (This book is for educational use and not prescriptive healthcare treatment.) I grew up thinking that treasures were a myth and that people who sought them were on a wild goose chase. My attitude and thinking about treasures were influenced by cartoons on television and books like *Treasure Island, Muppet Treasure Island,* and conversations with family and childhood friends. In the Treasure Island story, Captain Billy Bones dies, and the young boy takes off with the treasure map to find the treasure. But when he discovers the treasure chest and opens it, it is empty.

I have learned as an adult that treasures are not a myth, because people seek earthly and spiritual treasures in life. Those earthly treasures are temporal and can be anything a person values in the form of wealth—money, jewels, anything that confers material or personal status. But spiritual treasures are eternal and can be found only in God through our Lord and Savior Jesus Christ, who paid the price for all our sins.

It is in Christ Jesus that we learn to live abundantly. The Holy Spirit lives in us and empowers us to grow in the love, grace, and knowledge of our Lord Jesus Christ. You will see spiritual treasures working as we apply the Word of God in our daily lives. As we grow and mature in our Christian walk, spiritual treasures manifest because we trust and obey the word. Spiritual treasures display themselves in how we love God and take care of ourselves and care for others. Seeking earthly treasure as motivated by greed leads to disaster and failure, but seeking spiritual treasures in God's word as motivated by God's love leads to blessing and prosperity.

I encourage you to start journaling as you work through this book. A journal is a written record of your thoughts, experiences, and observations. You can write in your journal when you feel the urge to capture a thought or when you want to consider and respond to something you have read or learned. Journaling is an exercise that can help us become more aware of ourselves and our surroundings in life. I have provided space for journaling within the book, as well as some extra blank pages at the end to record your notes. So for the next month, I challenge you to start journaling, beginning with chapter 2 and continuing with one chapter a week through chapter 5, applying the "nuggets" and answering these "Key Thinking and Action Questions" for each chapter:

1. What main nugget captured your thought?
2. What nugget(s) inspired change?
3. What self-centered things will you consider letting go, and what God-centered things will you consider pursuing or adopting?

When you finish reading *Nuggets for the Soul*, my prayer is that on this journey called life you find yourself hopeful, healthier, loved, resilient, surprised, nourished, joyful, and honored for the gift you are to God, yourself, and others. In Jesus name!

> Beloved, I wish above all things that thou may prosper and be in health, even as thy soul prospereth. (3 John 1:2)

1

The Genesis of the Soul

The Lord God formed man of the dust of the
ground, and breathed into his nostrils the breath
of life, and man became a living soul.

Genesis 2:7

The *Holman Bible Dictionary* defines the study of human
beings, in Christian theology called "the doctrine of man,"
as a comprehensive examination of all aspects of human
existence. Biblical anthropology studies the portrait of
human beings, male and female, in scripture.

The term *anthropology* comes from two Greek words,
anthropos, meaning "man" (a human of either sex), and
logos, meaning "word, talk, or discussion of underlying
principles." We use the term *anthropology* to refer to the
social scientific study of humans, and *biblical anthropology*

to refer to the study of humans as understood primarily from scripture.

In the context of Christian theology, anthropology focuses on the human in relation to God. This theological approach differs from the social science of anthropology, which primarily deals with the comparative study of the physical and social characteristics of humanity across cultures, times, and places.[1] Thus Christian anthropology often involves discussing the human creation in the "image of God" (Genesis 1:27), the constitutional nature of humanity, and humanity after the fall.[2] Made in the image of God, the human is a living soul (Genesis 1:26–27; 2:7; Isaiah 45:12).

The human person is a tripartite (threefold) being, as described in figure 1. According to Reverend Clarence Larkin,[3]

a. the human is a spirit (John 3:6; 1 Corinthians 2:11, 6:17; Roman 8:16)

b. the human has a soul (Hebrews 4:12; Mark 8:36, 12:30)

c. the human lives in a body (1 Corinthians 6:19–20, 9:27; James 2:26)

[1] Wikipedia, s.v. "Christian Anthropology," accessed February 5, 2022, https://en.wikipedia.org/wiki/Christian_anthropology

[2] Bible.org, "Anthropology-Hamartiology" accessed February 5, 2022, https://bible.org/seriespage/5-anthropology-hamartiology-man-and-sin

[3] Clarence Larkin, *Dispensational Truth* (Glenside, PA: Rev. Clarence Larkin Publishers, 1918) 99. Used with permission of the Rev. Clarence Larkin Estate, PO Box 334, Glenside, PA 19038, www.larkinestate.com.

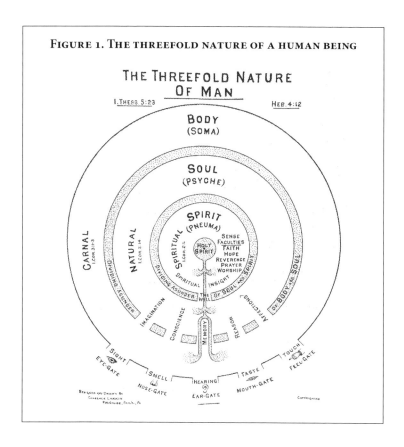

FIGURE 1. THE THREEFOLD NATURE OF A HUMAN BEING

The origin of anything is an important place to start. Figure 1 is helpful in showing that we are more than our spirits and souls, and much more than our bodies, but every element is essential.

Salvation in the Threefold Nature of Human Beings

There are three processes in salvation: justification, sanctification, and glorification. Each process targets a specific area of the threefold nature.

- The first process is *justification*, and it occurs in the spirit part of you the moment you accept Jesus Christ as Lord of your life. You have become born again and made spiritually alive in your spirit by the Holy Spirit. This process empowers us to communicate and connect with God as new believers.
- The second process is *sanctification*, and it occurs in the soul part of you. This progressive process begins with knowing and understanding that you are becoming saved in your soul from the power of sin and becoming more Christlike.
- The third process is *glorification*, and it occurs in the physical body when we die or when the Lord returns. The physical body is saved and puts on a new glorified body, which is the heavenly body that lives eternally with God.

In summary, the Holy Spirit changed and renewed the spirit man. Christ will save and change the body in glory. But the soul part of a person progressively becomes like Jesus, depending on how information is obtained and thought about and judgments formed to make decisions that align with the Holy Spirit. The soul part of a person is the area we are responsible for working on until we die or until the Lord returns.

2

The Biblical Characteristics of the Soul

What is the soul? According to the *Vines Complete Expository Dictionary*, the Hebrew word נֶפֶשׁ, *nephesh*, although translated as "soul" in some older English Bibles, has a meaning closer to "living being." The Hebrew word *nephesh* is a key Old Testament term that occurs over 780 times. *Nephesh* is rendered in the Septuagint as ψυχή (*psūchê*), the Greek word for "soul," "the breath," and "the breath of life."

The New Testament term *psūchê* or *psyche* occurs 102 times. The term *psyche* moves away from the Old Testament sense of the "breath of life" and includes the idea of body, flesh, and spirit to characterize human existence. In the Bible, the body and soul (or spirit) are not opposite terms but rather terms that supplement each other to describe aspects of the inseparable whole person (as seen in figure 1, "The Threefold Nature of a Human Being").

The *Vines Complete Expository Dictionary* defines the soul as the seat of the emotions and feelings; mind, conscious and unconscious; and will, desires, and affections:

- **emotions,** any nervousness of the feelings actuated by experiencing love, hate, fear, and so forth, and usually accompanied by certain physiological changes, such as increased heartbeat, respiration, laughing, crying, shaking, and so on (Ecclesiastes 3:8, 7:9; 2 Corinthians 4:7–10; 1 Timothy 6:3–5; 2 Timothy 2:24; James 3:13–18)
- **mind,** the element that provides intellect or understanding, as distinguished from the facilities of feeling and willing (Mark 12:30; Romans 7:23, 8:7, 12:1–2; Philippians 2:5; Isaiah 26:3; Ezekiel 11:5; 1 Peter 3:8; 4:1)
- **will,** the faculty of conscious and deliberate action, the power of control the mind has over its actions and freedom of the will (1 John 2:16); for example, *sinful* will (Adam and Eve's lust of the eye, Genesis 3:6; David's lust of the flesh, 2 Samuel 11:2–4; and Nebuchadnezzar's pride of life, Daniel 4:1–18) versus *submitted* will (Joshua 24:15; Luke 22:42; James 4:7)

The soul gives a human personality, self-awareness, rationality, and natural feeling.

Why Should We Care about Our Souls?

There are four main reasons to care about the soul.

1. The lives of our souls affect the health of our spirits and physical bodies: "Beloved, I wish above all things that thou mayest prosper and be in health, even as thy soul prospereth" (3 John 1:2).

2. We were created to bring God glory in the earth as it is in heaven: "Even everyone that is called by my name: for I have created him for my glory, I have formed him; yea, I have made him" (Isaiah 43:7). Here are two other ways to put it:

    You're here to be light, bringing out the God-colors in the world. God is not a secret to be kept. We're going public with this, as public as a city on a hill. If I make you light bearers, you don't think I'm going to hide you under a bucket, do you? I'm putting you on a light stand. Now that I've put you there on a hilltop, on a light stand—shine! Keep open house; be generous with your lives. By opening to others, you'll prompt people to open up to God, this generous Father in heaven. (Matthew 5:14–16 MSG)

> Thou art worthy, O Lord, to receive glory and honour and power: for thou hast created all things, and for thy pleasure, they are and were created. (Revelation 4:11)

3. All souls belong to Him: "Behold, all souls are mine; as the soul of the father, so also the soul of the son is mine: the soul that sinneth, it shall die" (Ezekiel 18:4).

4. The condition of one's soul prepares a person for the coming of the Lord and eternal life: "He that believeth on the Son hath everlasting life: and he that believeth not on the Son shall not see life; but the wrath of God abideth on him" (John 3:36). Accepting Jesus as our personal Savior allows us to live now and eternally.

Statistics show that self-healing and self-care are popular and seem to be the norm in our society today. According to current online market reviews, in 2014 the estimated value of the self-care market was $10 billion but has increased to $450 billion as health and wellness trends rise.[4] Included in this market are items such as exercise gadgets, skincare

---

[4] Macala Wright, "What Self-Care Trends Mean for Retailers In 2022," ASD Market Week, accessed November 16, 2021, https://asdonline.com/blog/retail-news/what-self-care-trends-mean-for-retailers-in-2020/; IRI, "Taking Charge: Consumers Grabbing Hold of Their Health and Wellness Drives $450-Billion Opportunity" (November 2018), accessed November 16, 2021, https://www.iriworldwide.com/IRI/media/Library/Publications/IRI_Self_Care_POV.pdf.

products, food, vitamins, spa treatments, and vacation resorts, each promising great results. Unfortunately, I found that there are not many items or books available for soul care compared to self-care, because the market seems to view self-care as being soul-care.

Soul care does not seem commonly expected, nor is it the focus even in many congregations today. Back in the eighties, the saints of old would cry out in prayer, "Lord save my soul." Nowadays, people are crying out for physical needs, healings, money, financial favor on the job, promotions in the church, and so forth. I pray that we will once again in Christendom realize that the Lord is pleased when we focus on those things that matter to Him. Soul care is God-centered, but self-care is self-centered.

Build Up Your Soul

Consider the parable of the rich man.

> And he spake a parable unto them, saying, The ground of a certain rich man brought forth plentifully: … And I will say to my soul, Soul, thou hast many goods laid up for many years; take thine ease, eat, drink, and be merry. But God said unto him, Thou fool, this night thy soul shall be required of thee: then whose shall those things be, which

thou hast provided? So, is he that layeth up treasure for himself, and is not rich toward God? (Luke 12:16, 19–21)

Unfortunately, the rich man spent his time building earthly wealth and failed to focus on building up his soul. This parable reminds us that our souls are eternally important to God: "What does it profit a man to gain the world and lose his soul?" (Mark 8:36). When we become aware of why we should care about our souls, we will look at our lives differently and understand that how we live daily will determine our eternal destiny.

The Bible teaches us that life in Christ Jesus is the one gift that makes all things possible: "For in Him, we live, and move and have our being; as certain also of your poets have said, for we are also his offspring" (Acts 17:28). In Him, we can make the most of every minute despite the challenges, triumphs, setbacks, successes, and moments of happiness, disappointment, delight, joy, and prosperity.

Over the past fifty years, several studies have been conducted that show a person's health and well-being benefit when their spiritual needs are addressed.[5] [6]

---

[5] Christina M. Puchalski, MD, MS "The role of spirituality in healthcare" NCBI (October 2001) accessed February 5, 2022, https://www.ncbi.nlm.nih.gov/pmc/articles/PMC1305900/

[6] Nell Cockell, MA, Cantab, BDiv, "Spiritual care in nursing: an overview of published international research" Wiley Online Library (October 15, 2012) accessed February 5, 2022 https://onlinelibrary.wiley.com/doi/abs/10.1111/j.1365-2834.2012.01450.x

Spiritual needs and concerns usually relate to what we call the "big" questions of life. Most people ask these questions in various ways during their lives, especially when they realize there is more to life; they could be better, or they feel they are not prospering. In addition, people may ask these questions when someone they love is sick or when they themselves are in a crisis and feeling wounded because of a loss, disappointment, rejection, abandonment, offense, abuse (mental and physical), or even misunderstandings.[7]

Nugget for thought and application: Do you have any big questions about your life? Use the questions below as a worksheet to begin journaling your thoughts, experiences, and observations.

The "big" questions of life may include:

- Why is this happening? Why is it happening to me?
- What does it all mean?
- How do I make sense of everything?
- How do I feel about changes in my life?
- What gives me comfort and hope?
- What do I call "good" in my life? What do I call "bad"?

---

[7] UMMC, "What is Spiritual Care? (June, 12, 2018) accessed February 5, 2022, https://www.umms.org/ummc/patients-visitors/for-patients/pastoral-care/what-is-spiritual-care

- What am I grateful for?
- What do I trust? Whom do I trust?
- Who is my "beloved community"? Who loves me and is loved by me, no matter what?
- What or who, beyond myself, do I believe is important in my life?

Do You Know Your Soul?

Let's begin our treasure hunt for soul nuggets by taking a short self-assessment to see how well you know your soul (mind, will, and emotions).

Do you know your soul?	
YOUR MIND	What do you spend your time thinking about? *(Sports, the latest movie, the latest gossip, the job, the Word of God, the children, or—?)*

YOUR WILL	How do you make choices and decisions? *(Based on how you feel, without thought, on information studied, on the spot, based on experience, the Word of God ...?)*
YOUR EMOTIONS	Are you quick to laugh and smile or to cry, or to be angry, disappointed, sad, or happy? Or is it up and down? *(For example, when plans change, promises are broken, or prayer is not answered)*

3

Nuggets for the Mind

The mind is self-awareness, the seat of reflective consciousness, the faculty of knowing and understanding. Is your mind the same as your brain? No!

- The brain is a tangible organ, and the mind is intangible, as in consciousness.
- The brain has blood vessels and nerve cells; the mind does not.
- The brain is lodged in the skull and has a definite shape; the mind does not.
- The brain is the center of the nervous system; it performs definite functions such as coordinating movement, feelings, and thoughts. The mind initiates comprehension and perception and relates to an individual's thought process.

The United Negro College Fund's slogan is "A mind is a terrible thing to waste," and that remains true today. This organization has helped many African Americans come out of poverty and become successful because they received an education opportunity. Some successful recipients include Dr. Martin Luther King, civil rights activist; Spike Lee, movie director; Samuel L. Jackson, actor; and my former bishop, Charles E. Blake, presiding bishop, Church of God in Christ.

If wrong information or no information comes into our thoughts, you can expect little to no good results. My grandmother would often tell us, when we had watched cartoons or comedy shows too long, that "an idle mind is the devil's workshop." She nicely told us to turn off the television and get out our schoolbook or the Bible to read something wholesome. Hanging around on the front porch doing nothing was considered a form of daydreaming that often led to mischief. So when we put the correct information in our thoughts, we shape our lives to do, choose, and respond in a good way.

Mindfulness

Mindfulness is being aware and present at all times. Being present and mindful is an intentional act to recognize and notice our surroundings and thoughts.

Have you ever driven or walked somewhere and later realized that you did not notice a person or a particular landmark? We often have a daily routine and do not always pay attention to the details around us. Lacking awareness of the present, past, and future can impact the health of the soul. So we must awaken and know the Word, will, and ways of God for our lives.

> Wherefore he saith, Awake thou that sleepest, and rise from the dead, and Christ shall give thee light. (Ephesians 5:14)

Nugget 1: Embrace God. Live life.

As we embrace God, accepting the Word, will, values, desires, and ways of God for our lives, we become renewed, and our minds transformed.

> If ye abide in me, and my words abide in you, ye shall ask what ye will, and it shall be done unto you. (John 15:7)

Our souls are awakened to finding out more about God's will concerning our thoughts, decisions, emotions, and situations.

> Be ye transformed by the renewing of your mind, that ye may prove what is that good,

and acceptable, and perfect, will of God. (Romans 12:2b)

When we intentionally decide to yield to the Lord, it will get easier, becoming a habit and enjoyable.

> As newborn babes, desire the sincere milk of the word, that ye may grow thereby; if so be ye have tasted that the Lord is gracious. (1 Peter 2:1–2)

Change and Transformation

Over time, we condition our brains to doing certain things a certain way. To get different results, we must strategically change our way of doing things. You can change your life by changing your words. Changing our words, thoughts, and actions will begin to transform our lives. The scripture is clear: "Death and life are in the power of the tongue: And they that love it shall eat the fruit thereof" (Proverbs 18:21). Words determine our destiny.

Transformation and change are related but different. Change is the first step to transformation, but change alone is not transformation. You can change an approach or direction because change begins as a new set of behaviors. For example, you may change your choice of drink because it is harmful to your health, but when you go to the grocery store or are in a certain setting, you crave that same drink and purchase it for later. Out of habit, you begin drinking the same drink again because it is behavior-based.

Transformation happens when you no longer want the drink even though you may crave it. For me as a new babe in Christ, it was hard to quit smoking. I used to love to smoke cigarettes, but the more I read and meditated on the Word of God concerning my body being the temple of the Holy Spirit and what pleases God, the more I lost the taste and desire to smoke, and eventually I found myself a new set of behaviors that I applied to my daily life. Transformation is when your mind, will, and emotions lead you to go another way and make a different choice. It is also when you no longer have the desire for old habits and behaviors; you have now been transformed! The change has been long enough, deep enough, and effective enough to change your values and desires.

In other words, your desire to live your new life replaces the desire to live your old life: "And have put on the new man, which is renewed in the knowledge after the image of Him that created him" (Colossians 3:10a).

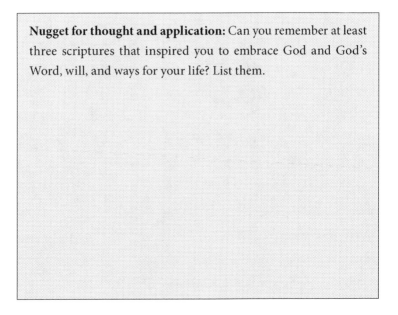

Nugget for thought and application: Can you remember at least three scriptures that inspired you to embrace God and God's Word, will, and ways for your life? List them.

Nugget 2: Let go. Discover your options.

Nelson Mandela stated, "as I walked out the door toward the gate that would lead to my freedom, I knew if I didn't leave my bitterness and hatred behind, I'd still be in prison." For a fresh start, *forgive* yourself and others; move forward in a new direction by how you treat yourself. Think about what you have learned, not what happened or what someone did to you. Next, think about what you want for yourself now and in the future. Write it down in your journal so you can see and think about what you desire. Finally, broaden your vision by thinking about what you can do for your spiritual, physical, and emotional health, your well-being, and your wealth. If it means changing your environment, friends, job, or school, do it to discover all your options.

Know Your Options

A professor stood in front of his class holding a sixteen-ounce bottle of water. He asked the students what would happen if he held the bottle for five minutes, and they replied, "Nothing." He asked whether his arm would tire if he held it for ten minutes in that position, and they replied, "Yes." He asked, "What about if I held it thirty minutes?" They said his arm would most likely begin to cramp. He said, "What about all day?" The class said it would hurt and become very painful.

When we hold on to the anger and disappointments other persons have caused us, or to our own weights and sins, they will not only hurt us but also immobilize and keep us from living a wholesome and prosperous life.

Years ago, a family in my community lost their teenage daughter unexpectedly. The mother's grief was devastating. She would visit her daughter's gravesite daily and sometimes sit, weep, and talk to her. The father and other siblings tried to console the mother, but she rejected them and others who tried to comfort her through the grief process. The mother's health began to deteriorate because of the grief, and she died prematurely.

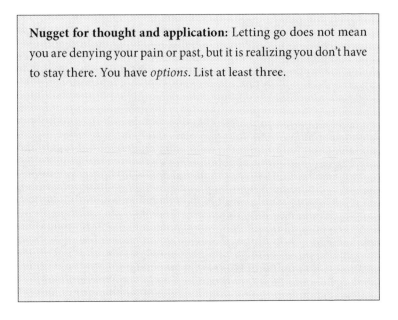

Nugget for thought and application: Letting go does not mean you are denying your pain or past, but it is realizing you don't have to stay there. You have *options*. List at least three.

Sometimes the thought of letting go of a painful past or incident or letting go of pleasurable things that have not been good for you can be grievous. According to Dictionary.com, *grief* is "keen mental suffering or distress over affliction or loss; sharp sorrow; painful regret." Grief is a natural response to losing someone or something important to you.

In 1969, Swiss psychiatrist Elisabeth Kuber-Ross introduced her five-stage grief model—denial, anger, bargaining, depression, and acceptance, popularly referred to as DABDA. Clinicians who use this model as a guide recognize that some people may go through all the stages, some of the stages, or possibly none of the five stages.

- **Denial** helps us to survive the shock of the loss.
- **Anger** is a necessary stage of feeling the loss. You are in the middle of the situation, and the more you experience how you feel, the sooner you can begin to heal.
- **Bargaining** is when the 'what if' thoughts and guilt feelings begin to surface. What if I had done this? Why didn't I see this coming? The 'what if' allows you to return to a place of acceptance.
- **Depression**, it is important to realize, is natural. This state is not a mental illness but the appropriate response to loss. The realization that someone will not come back again or that something will never be the same again is also part of the healing process.
- **Acceptance** is realizing that the loss has happened. It is most likely a permanent situation and a new reality. Finding acceptance can mean accepting there will be good days and bad days. We don't deny our feelings, but we listen to our needs; we move, we change, we grow, we evolve, and we begin to live again.

Nugget for thought and application: "Would you like to get well?" (John 5:6b NLT). Describe three specific actions you can take for your spiritual, physical, emotional health, and your well-being.

Nugget 3: Grow and become.

Growth requires work. As John Ruskin observed, "The highest reward for man's toil is not what he gets for it, but what he becomes by it." The farmer tills the ground to plant seeds for his crop so that he may have a great harvest. During the planting season, the farmer must be aware of the pest, insects, birds, and animals that come to dig up his seeds. If the farmer must be watchful and check his crops daily, we must also be watchful and aware of the enemies that attack our minds and thinking daily. Sometimes the farmer puts a net over the field; he puts things out to scare pests, or he may even use a spray that repels the insects. We, too, must protect and fortify our minds by yielding to the Word, will, and ways of God. Our enemy will try to bring back the old way of thinking and doing so he can take over.

> For though we walk in the flesh, we do not war after the flesh; For the weapons of our warfare are not carnal, but mighty through God to the pulling down of strongholds; Casting down imaginations, and every high thing that exalteth itself against the knowledge of God, and bringing into captivity every thought to the obedience of Christ. (2 Corinthians 10:3–5)

In other words, if your thinking goes against the Word of God, check it and cast it down, because the enemy is trying to rebuild his old house. If you accept it, the enemy will bring more trash, but when you reject it, you are fortifying and building up your new house with the Word of God.

> Therefore, whosoever heareth these sayings of mine, and doeth them, I will liken him unto a wise man, which built his house upon a rock. (Matthew 7:24)

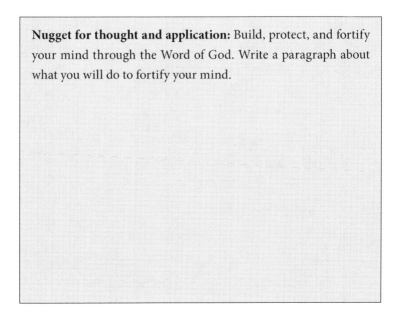

Nugget for thought and application: Build, protect, and fortify your mind through the Word of God. Write a paragraph about what you will do to fortify your mind.

I enjoyed reading Howard Thurman's book *Meditations of the Heart.* My professor in divinity school encouraged us to be more introspective and reflective in our thinking, and he often opened our class session with the meditation "How Good to Center Down!"

How good it is to center down!
To sit quietly and see oneself pass by!
The streets of our minds seethe with endless traffic;
Our spirits resound with clashings, with noisy silences …
We look at ourselves in this waiting moment-
what kinds of people we are.
How good it is to center down! [8]

---

[8] Howard Thurman, *Meditations of the Heart* (Boston: Beacon Press, 1981) 28.

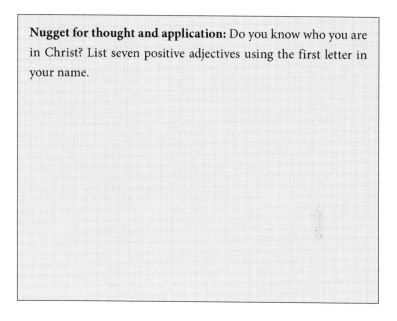

Nugget for thought and application: Do you know who you are in Christ? List seven positive adjectives using the first letter in your name.

Centering down forces you to look at yourself, what you like and dislike, your wounds, misunderstandings, and failures. It forces you to acknowledge that yes, it happened, and I am not happy about it. Centering down is also an excellent exercise that will help us to stay focused on what is important. It allows you to ask yourself, "Do I want to be whole?" in spirit, soul, and body.

Prioritize Time Alone with God

Capturing our thoughts require stillness: "Be still and know that I am God" (Psalm 46:10a). There are books, journal articles, magazine articles, and electronic resources on the benefits of meditation and prayer. Meditation and prayer were familiar and encouraged by the authors of the scriptures. Genesis 24:63 says, "And Isaac went out to meditate in the field in the evening." The Psalter calls all people to emulate the "blessed man" whose "delight is in the law of the Lord, and on His law, he meditates day and night. And whatsoever he doeth shall prosper" (Psalm 1:2–3). Jesus prioritized time alone with God (Mark 1:35) and sought places of solitude to pray and express His reliance on God (Luke 5:15–16).

We must also prioritize time alone with God and take time during the day to think. What are you thinking about? Pray about it, and then write it down in your journal. Take it out of your head and put it on paper where you can see it for what it is. Ask yourself, Is this about the present, past, or future, and do I have options? If so, what are they?

First, begin to search the scriptures, for "Thy word is a lamp unto my feet and a light unto my path" (Psalm 119:105). Second, find two or three scriptures that pertain to your concern or desire. Lay them before the Lord in prayer, and meditate on them (chew on them!) for two or three days. Next, start listing your options and taking the necessary actions to grow and become who the Lord God has called you to become.

Nugget for thought and application: Will I be honest, consistent, committed, and responsible in my pursuit of wholeness? Explain how.

Key Thinking and Action Questions:

1. What main nugget captured your thought?

2. What nugget(s) inspired change?

3. What self-centered things will you consider letting go, and what God-centered things will you consider pursuing or adopting?

4

Nuggets for the Will

The will is the faculty of conscious and deliberate action; rationality. Figure 2 shows how the soul can be governed and influenced by the Holy Spirit in the spiritual realm or by the external world, which is the physical realm and its five senses.

The will of Adam and Eve impacts their lives and obedience to God. They chose not to trust and obey God but to yield to the temptations of the tree—it was from the natural world and looked good, which is a reference to the lust of the eyes. God has made us all free will agents and given us the capacity to choose whom we will trust and obey. It was their choice, and so it is ours!\

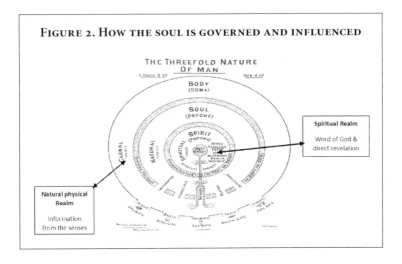

FIGURE 2. HOW THE SOUL IS GOVERNED AND INFLUENCED

Yield to the Spirit

Figure 2 gives us a clear picture of where and how the process works in the soul to make the right choices in life so that you have peace with God, yourself, and others. Scripture informs us,

> For they that are after the flesh do mind the things of the flesh; but they that are after the Spirit the things of the Spirit. For to be carnally minded is death; but to be spiritually minded is life and peace. Because the carnal mind is enmity against God: for it is not subject to the law of God, neither indeed can be. So, then they that are in the flesh cannot please God. (Romans 8:5–8)

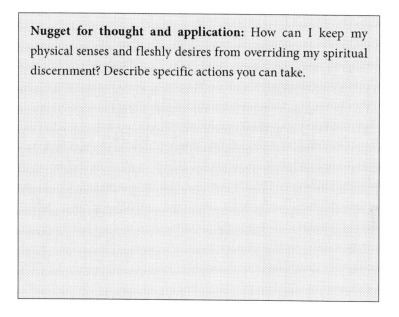

Nugget for thought and application: How can I keep my physical senses and fleshly desires from overriding my spiritual discernment? Describe specific actions you can take.

Nugget 1: Make a decision. Choose life.

> And if it seems evil unto you to serve the LORD, choose you this day whom ye will serve; whether the gods which your fathers served that were on the other side of the flood, or the gods of the Amorites, in whose land ye dwell: but as for me and my house, we will serve the Lord. (Joshua 25:15)

The free will to choose is another part of the soul that we have to prosper in the Lord and in life. According to the King

James Version Dictionary, *choice* is "the act of choosing; the voluntary act of selecting or separating from two or more things that is preferred; option; care in selecting; judgment or skill in distinguishing what is to be preferred, and in giving preference."

Figure 2 shows that if we grow in the knowledge of the Word of God, we become more sensitive to yielding to the Spirit of God and not to the physical world or fleshly desires. For example, toddlers are inquisitive and want to touch and eat practically everything they see, but parents, who know the danger, are responsible for teaching them. Many times, the parent will say no repeatedly, but it will not stop the toddler until the child has touched the hot dish or broken the figurine on the table. As we grow, observe, and experience the consequences and blessings of obeying our parents or following the rules at home, in school, on the playground, at work, or wherever, we begin to see life-changing results. Making the right choice is also empowering when you see the blessings of that decision manifested in your life.

The Holy Spirit is available and waiting to help us. Jesus said, "But when the Father sends the Advocate as my representative—that is, the Holy Spirit—he will teach you everything and will remind you of everything I have told you" (John 14:26 NLT).

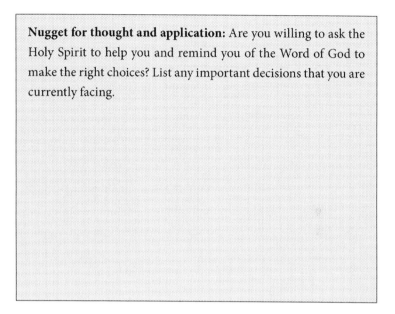

Nugget for thought and application: Are you willing to ask the Holy Spirit to help you and remind you of the Word of God to make the right choices? List any important decisions that you are currently facing.

Nugget 2: Pursue. Begin again.

Courage is a trait that everyone desires. However, courage is not simply bravery, and it is necessary to begin again when we make the wrong choice. Dragana Djukic has described six types of courage we may need to face life challenges as we begin again.[9]

1. **Physical courage,** feeling fear yet choosing to act, involves bravery at the risk of bodily harm or death

---

[9] Dragana Djukic, "The Six Types of Courage," Quantumkoan, accessed June 23, 2021, https://www.quantumkoan.com/the-six-types-of-courage/ and used by permission of the author.

and developing physical strength, resilience, and awareness.

2. **Emotional courage,** following our heart, opens us to feeling the full spectrum of emotions—pleasant and unpleasant—without attachment.

3. **Intellectual courage,** expanding our horizons and letting go of the familiar, is about our willingness to learn, unlearn, and relearn with an open and flexible mind.

4. **Social courage** to be ourselves in the face of adversity involves the risk of social embarrassment or exclusion, unpopularity, or rejection, as well as leadership.

5. **Moral courage,** standing up for what is right, involves doing the right thing even when it is uncomfortable or unpopular.

6. **Spiritual courage,** facing pain with dignity or faith, helps us live with purpose and meaning through a heart-centered approach towards all life and oneself.

As Aristotle said, "You will never do anything in this world without courage. It is the greatest quality of the mind next to honor."

Be Willing To Use It or Lose It

Matthew 25:14–30 is a familiar passage about talents that the Lord gave His servants. Talents represent our abilities, time, resources, and opportunities to serve God and others while we are on earth. We are responsible to administer them in the wisest way possible. God gave His servants talents in the amounts of five, two, and one, each according to their abilities. The one with the five talents used them and gained five more; the one with two used them and gained two more; but the one with the one talent decided never to use his, so he hid it in the ground. All three were given the ability and capacity to use what they had, but only two had the courage and faith in God to pursue the opportunity to multiply and utilize their talents. The Lord calls the one who buried his talent slothful and wicked because he chose not to use what he was given. The apostle Paul said, "Whether therefore ye eat, drink, or whatsoever ye do, do all to the glory of God" (1 Corinthians 10:31).

However, when I think about courage, I realize that one must be encouraged or inspired by someone or something to take courage. The two servants did not try to encourage or inspire the one servant to use his talent. Many times in life you will have to motivate yourself to take courage. I recall a time during my son's first year in college at the University of Maryland Eastern Shore when I received a call from him, saying that he needed my signature immediately to receive additional financial aid. I was frightened and scared out of my wits to drive over the Bay Bridge alone, since my husband had to work. I was very proud of my son for wanting to attend college, so I had to pray and think about why I had to drive over and this long bridge and back. I was inspired and happy because he was in college, and I did not want to cause him to drop out, so I went to sign his financial aid paperwork. After that trip to the university, the other trips got easier and enjoyable. I would have regretted being the cause of his missing a semester because I would not take the courage to overcome my fear of driving across the Bay Bridge. One of my favorite sayings is, the only way to silence regret is to pursue it, whatever it is!

Nugget for thought and application: list in order of priority three goals you want to accomplish that will bring glory to God and bless you and others.

Nugget 3: Never give up.
Hope in the Lord.

> Be of good courage, and he shall strengthen your heart,
> all ye that hope in the Lord.
>
> Psalm 31:24

In Matthew 25:25, the servant gives the reason he hides his talent: "I was afraid, and went and hid thy talent in the earth." This condition of fear can cause symptoms and actions of doubt. Fear is an emotion induced by perceived danger or threat, which causes physiological changes and ultimately behavioral changes such as doubt.

False
Evidence
Appearing
Real

Doubt is a feeling of uncertainty, hesitation, reservation, and distrust. Fear and doubt are bad conditions, if allowed to gain control and build a stronghold. The spirit of fear is defined in Romans 8:15 as a spirit of bondage.

Faith Is a Muscle You Must Use

Every believer has been given a measure of faith, according to Romans 12:3, so we do not have to accept these conditions of fear and doubt when we exercise our faith in God. The message of God is called the word of faith: "But what saith it? The word is nigh thee, even in thy mouth, and in thy heart: that is, the word of faith, which we preach" (Romans 10:8). Our faith will increase as we trust, believe, and apply the Word of God to our lives. Faith is like a muscle—the more you exercise it, the stronger your faith will grow in God.

There are three principles to notice in Mark 11:22–23 about faith in God.

1. Believe with your heart.
2. Believe with your words.
3. Believe with your actions.

To have the victory, we must act on what we say and believe. The two servants in Matthew 25:14–30 believed what was spoken and acted. Yes, it takes courage and faith in God to make the right choices in life. As Oswald Chambers observed, "The great thing about faith in God is that it keeps man undisturbed amid disturbance."

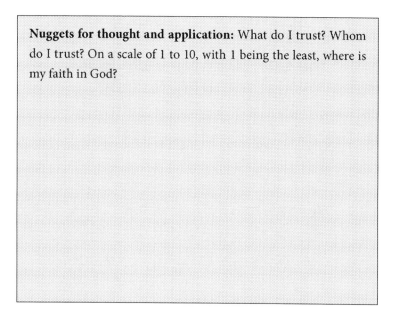

Nuggets for thought and application: What do I trust? Whom do I trust? On a scale of 1 to 10, with 1 being the least, where is my faith in God?

I call heaven and earth to record this day against you,
that I have set before you, life and death, blessing and
cursing;
therefore, choose life, that both thou
and thy seed may live.
Deuteronomy 30:19

Key Thinking and Action Questions:

1. What main nugget captured your thought?

2. What nugget(s) inspired change?

3. What self-centered things will you consider letting go, and what God-centered things will you consider pursuing or adopting?

5

Nuggets for the Emotions

Merriam-Webster defines emotion as "a conscious mental reaction such as anger, pleasure, joy, or fear, experienced as strong feeling usually directed toward a specific object and typically accompanied by physiological and behavioral changes in the body such as increased heartbeat, respiration, laughing, crying, shaking, etc.; a state of feeling".

God cares about how and why we feel happy, sad, or angry, as well as the way we feel and how we react or respond. God said to Cain: "Why this tantrum? Why the sulking? If you do well, won't you be accepted? And if you don't do well, sin is lying in wait for you, ready to pounce; it's out to get you, you've got to master it" (Genesis 4:6-7 MSG)

We Are Responsible for Our Emotions

As a young adult, I wanted to attend a party with a boyfriend who lived in another county. I did not have a license to drive nor a car to meet him, so I took my mother's car and went to the party while she was asleep. Late that night, I brought the car back and parked it in the driveway. I thought, I made it back home, and I did not get caught. When I got out of the vehicle, it rolled into the side of our house and woke her up. I realized I forgot to put the emergency brake on! The car was not damaged, but the cost of that date and joyride to the party was not worth the punishment I received.

Whether emotions are positive or negative, we are accountable and pay the price for what we do with them. God has given human the capacity to rule over their fleshly emotions when they yield in faith to Christ Jesus and guidance from the Holy Spirit. In verse 8 in the passage from Genesis above, Cain failed to hear and yield to God's warning concerning his anger, so in anger he slew his brother, Abel, and in verse 16 Cain was driven out from the presence of the Lord.

Managing Our Emotions Is Healthy

Self-monitoring is an excellent strategy to build resilience while managing our emotions and feelings. It allows us to think and choose the correct response or reaction. According to Christiane Northrup, MD, "It has now been scientifically documented those specific patterns of emotional vulnerability can adversely affect organs or systems of the body. Conversely, emotional resilience in these same areas shores up health."[10] Self-monitoring also enables us to be intentional when we measure our emotions and feelings against the Word of God. It sets the tone for direction and guidance in our lives. Could our emotions and feelings be navigators, like the GPS that helps us on this life journey?

As Samuel Johnson advised, "Knock the 'T' off the word 'can't'."

> My son, attend to my words; incline thine ear, unto my sayings. Let them not depart from thine eyes; keep them in the midst of thine heart. For they are life unto those that find them, and health to all their flesh. (Proverbs 4:21–22)

Nugget 1: Check it.

"Check it" simply means "be aware and alert." Life happens, and if we are not aware, we will respond based on past

---

[10] Christiane Northrup, MD, *The Wisdom of Menopause: Creating Physical and Emotional Health during Change* (New York: Bantam Books, 2012) 58.

experiences. However, with time we can learn, as instructed in Proverbs 4:21–22, to self-monitor by being attentive. Our feelings and emotions can reveal either a healthy response or a warning to a negative reaction.

Experience has taught us that sometimes our emotions and feelings can lead us to make bad decisions. Feelings are not always facts; as demonstrated in the Cain and Abel story, emotions can cause wrong reactions to a preconceived situation and destroy relationships if unchecked.

Let's look at Galatians, chapter 5, where good and bad emotions and feelings are listed that we can use to help us check our responses and reactions to ensure they align themselves with a godly character:

> Now the works of the flesh are manifest, which are these; Adultery, fornication, uncleanness, lasciviousness, Idolatry, witchcraft, hatred, variance, emulations, wrath, strife, seditions, heresies, Envyings, murders, drunkenness, revellings, and such like: of the which I tell you before, as I have also told you in time past, that they which do such things shall not inherit the kingdom of God. But the fruit of the Spirit is love, joy, peace, longsuffering, gentleness, goodness, faith, Meekness, temperance: against such there is no law" (Galatians 5:19–23)

My pastor, Bishop James Jordan Jr., tells a Cherokee story about a hunter who brings his two wolves to town to compete in a dogfight. The story illustrates a moral lesson in managing our conduct, feelings, emotions, and actions.

> One evening, a Cherokee elder was teaching his grandson about life.
> "A fight is going on inside me," he said to the boy. "It is a terrible fight, and it is between two wolves. This battle that goes on between the two wolves is inside us all.
> "One wolf is Evil. He is anger, envy, jealousy, sorrow, regret, greed, arrogance, self-pity, guilt, resentment, inferiority, lies, false pride, superiority, and ego."
> He continued, "The other is Good. He is joy, peace, love, hope, serenity, humility, kindness, benevolence, empathy, generosity, truth, compassion, and faith."
> The grandson thought about it for a minute and then asked his grandfather: "Which wolf will win?"
> Wisely, the grandfather simply smiled and replied, "The one you feed." [11]

---

[11] Brian Scott, "The Story of the Two Wolves: Managing Your Thoughts, Feelings and Actions," PsychologyMatters.Asia, accessed July 7, 2021, https://www.psychologymatters.asia/article/65/the-story-of-the-two-wolves-managing-your-thoughts-feelings-and-actions.html

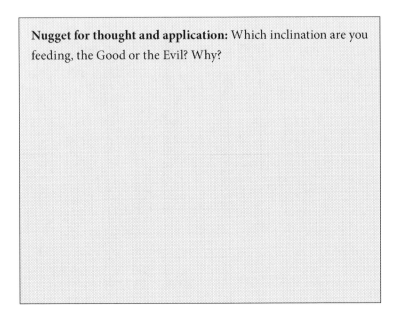

Nugget for thought and application: Which inclination are you feeding, the Good or the Evil? Why?

Nugget 2: Reflect on it. Correct it.

Now that we have become aware of our emotions and feelings, we can learn how to see them and understand them for what they are. For example, when you respond with love, peace, or joy, stop and ask yourself why. When you respond with contention, anger, and envy, stop and ask yourself why. Why did this situation or experience trigger this response? Is it an indicator pointing to a truth you may or may not like dealing with, or is it because of something else you had not realized before?

I am sure at some point you have said to yourself, "What was I thinking?" or "I could have handled this differently."

You may have felt "This blessed me," or "I love it when that happens," or "That was funny." All of these responses are valuable and useful in becoming transparent in order to assess and correct an attitude, emotion, or feeling.

Take it to God in prayer. God admonishes us to cast our cares upon Him because He loves us. In prayer we yield our thoughts or emotions unto God. Prayer is also a form of worship; it is a sacred and precious time for God to bring to your remembrance the things He has shown you in His Word and the things that He has done for you.

Philippians 4 admonishes us:

> Don't fret or worry. Instead of worrying, pray. Let petitions and praises shape your worries into prayers, letting God know your concerns. Before you know it, a sense of God's wholeness, everything coming together for good, will come and settle you down. It's wonderful what happens when Christ displaces worry at the center of your life. (Philippians 4:6–7 MSG)

Mindfulness and Discretion

Pastor Tony Evans shares a great illustration of why we need to be always mindful of our emotions and feelings.

In courthouses, you see policemen on post to keep the peace. The fact that a judge may have made you upset by ruling against you does not change the fact that you must behave respectfully in the courtroom and stay in your seat. Your feelings of frustration do not justify an emotional response or reason to cause chaos in the courtroom. You must control yourself. Why? Because if you don't, the policemen have the backing of the law to make you behave. Your feelings have to adjust to the reality of where you are. [12]

In the same way, we must measure our feelings and emotions against the reality of God's Word. His Word, and not our feelings, sets the tone for how we live: "When wisdom entereth into thine heart and knowledge is pleasant unto thy soul; Discretion shall preserve thee, understanding shall keep thee" (Proverbs 2:10–11).

Discretion is the quality of being discreet, especially with reference to one's own actions or speech. As children we have said, "Sticks and stones may break my bones, but words will never hurt me." But as adults, we know that words do hurt, and they stay with us for years to come. Discretion

---

[12] Tony Evans, *Tony Evans' Book of Illustrations* (Chicago: Moody Publishers, 2009) 83–84.

with our words and attitude is especially important for a Christian. Christians are to be Christlike and exemplify the teachings of Christ in their lives. A mature Christian will not let their mood and feelings take over their attitude or mouth.

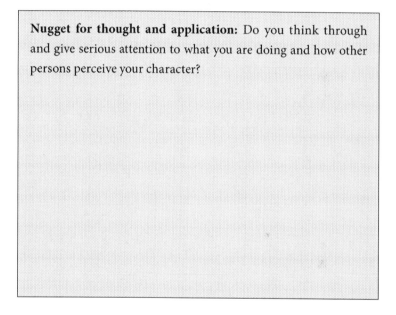

Nugget for thought and application: Do you think through and give serious attention to what you are doing and how other persons perceive your character?

Nugget 3: Be Refreshed. Bless.

Now let's consider our words, because they are a manifestation of our feelings and emotions. What are we saying to ourselves, to one another, and to God? Are they words that bless or curse?

Out of the same mouth proceeds blessing and cursing. My brethren, these things ought not to be. (James 3:10)

The *Vines Complete Expository Dictionary* defines the word *bless* as "good speaking, praise," as it is used in reference to God and Christ: "Worthy is the Lamb who was slain to receive power and riches wisdom, and strength and honor and glory and blessing" (Revelations 5:12). *Bless* also means to express or desire a wish of happiness to someone: "Isaac called Jacob and blessed him" (Genesis 28:1); to make happy or successful: "the Lord thy God shall bless thee in all thou doest" (Deuteronomy 15:18), so that to be blessed is to be favored, to prosper ("we are blessed with peace and plenty"); and to consecrate by prayer or invoke a blessing upon: "and Jesus took the five loaves and the two fish and looking up to heaven he blessed them" (Luke 9).

Words of blessings can be powerful opportunities to declare God's truth about Him, ourselves, and others. Be intentional. Be purpose-minded. Speak a blessing over the lives of everyone you meet. The next time you come across a person less fortunate, stop and bless them with your words. You may not have time or money, but you can always bless someone with a kind word. When you are kind to others, you help yourself, and when you are unkind to others, you are unkind to yourself.

Let the words of my mouth, and the
meditation of my heart, be acceptable in
thy sight, O Lord, my strength, and my
redeemer. (Psalms 19:14)

Nugget for thought and application: Always mind your p's and
q's. Write a prayer asking God to help you grow in discernment
and discretion.

Words Matter

John 15 is an excellent chapter that describes the results of
our relationship when it remains in fellowship and harmony
with Jesus Christ. In verses 7–9, Jesus says to the disciples,
"If ye abide in me, and my words abide in you, ye shall ask
what ye will, and it shall be done unto you. Herein is my
Father glorified, that ye bear much fruit; so, shall ye be my
disciples. As the Father hath loved me so have I loved you;
continue ye in my love."

In this text, it is important to note that abiding in
Christ gives us the privilege to "ask what we will" so that
the Father is glorified and we bear much fruit. Our words
matter, and they determine the type and amount of fruit
we bear. Whatever we sow, it will grow: "Be not deceived;
God is not mocked; for whatsoever a man soweth, that
shall he also reap" (Galatians 6:7). When we sow cursing
and negativity, we will see the fruit thereof, and when

we sow blessings and positivity, we will see the fruit of that also. However, scripture teaches us that learning to bless is best! Several individuals have been instrumental in my life and taught me how to encourage others in the Lord. On Sundays after church, the missionaries and deacons would allow me and my husband to go with them to visit the sick in the hospitals. Initially, we were allowed only to watch, but after a while they allowed us to read scripture and pray. Two or three years later, my husband became a deacon and I a missionary. The on-site training received during our hospital visits with the sick prepared us to minister alone to them. Attending Sunday school also helped us if we needed clarity because you could ask questions and learn from your classmates' questions.

When we receive uplifting, kind, and life-giving words, it lifts our spirit and encourages us to be tender and kindhearted to others.

The Lord God hath given me the tongue of the learned, that I should know how to speak a word in season to him that is weary: he wakeneth morning by morning, he awakeneth my ear to hear as the learned. (Isaiah 50:5)

Learning to speak words of blessings will refresh your soul, as the scriptures perpetually remind us.

The Lord bless you and keep you; the Lord make his face shine on you and be gracious to you; the Lord turn his face toward you and give you peace. (Numbers 6:24–26)

O my soul, bless God. From head to toe, I'll bless his holy name! O my soul, bless God, don't forget a single blessing. (Psalm 103:1–2 MSG)

Blessed are the undefiled in the way, who walk in the law of the Lord. Blessed are they that keep his testimonies and that seek him with the whole heart. (Psalms 119:1–2)

The one who blesses others is abundantly blessed: those who help others are helped. (Proverbs 11:25 MSG)

Bless those who persecute you; don't curse them: pray that God will bless them. (Romans 12:14 NLT)

The heart of the wise teacheth his mouth and addeth learning to his lips. Pleasant words are as a honeycomb, sweet to the soul, and health to the bones. (Proverbs 16:23–24)

Nugget for thought and application: Always W.A.T.C.H.:

Watch your **Words.**
Watch your **Actions.**
Watch your **Thoughts.**
Watch your **Companions.**
Watch your **Habits.** (adapted from Frank Outlaw)

Key Thinking and Action Questions:

1. What main nugget captured your thought?

2. What nugget(s) inspired change?

3. What self-centered things will you consider letting go, and what God-centered things will you consider pursuing or adopting?

6

Your Soul Matters

Having purified your souls by your obedience to the truth for a sincere brotherly love, love one another earnestly from a pure heart, since you have been born again, not of perishable seed but of imperishable, through the living and abiding word of God; for All flesh is like grass and all its glory like the flower of grass. The grass withers, and the flower falls, but the word of the Lord remains forever. (1 Peter 1:22–25)

Value your soul; it has a purpose in life. The soul is fundamental in the creation of humanity. Our lives are empowered through and by the Word of God spoken to this aspect of our being. God has already chosen a path that leads us to abundance, prosperity, and eternal life. I don't recall where I first heard this line, but it has remained with me for years: "No word, no power; little word, little power; more word, more overcoming power" (author unknown). I hope that *Nuggets for the Soul* has been a small treasure from the Word of God that gives you practical living tips and strategies that help transform your mind, will, and emotions. In this transformation, our souls are being purified and becoming Christlike.

> But if we walk in the light, God himself being the light, we also experience a shared life with one another, as the sacrificed blood of Jesus, God's Son, purges all our sin. (1 John 1:7 MSG)

Abba Father, I bless your name for the nuggets of life that make the soul whole. In Jesus name.

Suggested Readings

Howard Thurman, *Meditations of the Heart*

Dr. Caroline Leaf, *Cleaning Up Your Mental Mess*

Pastor Tony Evans, *Book of Illustrations*

John C. Maxwell, *Thinking for change*

Christiane Northrup, *The Wisdom of Menopause: Creating Physical and Emotional Health During Change*

Henri J.M. Nouwen, *Life of the Beloved*

Richard J. Foster, *Celebration of Discipline*

Notes

Notes

Notes

Notes

Notes

Notes

Notes

Notes

Notes

Notes

Notes

Notes

Notes

Notes

Notes

Notes

Notes

Notes

Notes

Notes

Notes

Notes

Notes

Notes

Notes

Notes

Printed in the United States
by Baker & Taylor Publisher Services